THE CRUISE
DIARY

THIS DIARY BELONGS TO

_____

AND RECORDS THE VOYAGE

_____

ON THE SHIP

_____

FROM_____TO_____ 19 _____

THE CRUISE
DIARY

RAINCOAST BOOKS
Vancouver

First published in 1997 by
Raincoast Books
8680 Cambie Street
Vancouver, B.C.
V6P 6M9
(604) 323-7100

10 9 8 7 6 5 4 3 2 1

CANADIAN CATALOGUING IN PUBLICATION DATA

Main entry under title:

The cruise diary

ISBN 1-55192-081-6

1. Diaries (Blank-books) 2. Ocean travel – Miscellanea.
G550.C78 1997 910'.2'02 C96-910844-3

Designed by Dean Allen
Edited by Michael Carroll
Maps: Michael Bender
Cover Photography: Tony Stone Images

Printed and bound in Canada

TABLE OF CONTENTS

SHIP'S TOUR

CRUISE LINE _____

SHIP _____

CAPTAIN _____

DOCTOR _____

CABIN STEWARD _____

DINING ROOM STEWARD _____

SHORE EXCURSION MANAGER _____

CRUISE DIRECTOR _____

CHIEF PURSER _____

HEAD WAITER _____

WINE STEWARD _____

SECOND WAITER _____

CHAPLAIN _____

CABIN _____

DECK _____

TYPE OF SHIP _____

YEAR COMMISSIONED _____

SHIP DETAILS _____

(size, etc.) _____

_____

_____

_____

RESTAURANTS _____

_____

_____

_____

LOUNGES AND NIGHTCLUBS _____

_____

_____

DATE OF DEPARTURE _____

DATE OF RETURN _____

PORT OF EMBARKATION _____

PORT OF DISEMBARKATION _____

SHIPBOARD ACTIVITIES _____

_____

_____

_____

_____

_____

_____

OTHER NOTES _____

_____

_____

_____

_____

_____

_____

_____

_____

_____

_____

_____

_____

_____

_____

_____

PERSONAL DATA

NAME _____

ADDRESS AND PHONE _____

_____

_____

_____

IN CASE OF EMERGENCY, _____

PLEASE CONTACT _____

_____

_____

_____

MEDICAL INSURANCE POLICY _____

GROUP # _____

FAMILY PHYSICIAN _____

PHONE NUMBER _____

BLOOD GROUP _____

SPECIAL MEDICAL INFO _____

(allergies, etc.) _____

_____

_____

RELIGION _____

S.I.N./SOCIAL SECURITY # _____

PASSPORT NUMBER _____

TICKET NUMBERS _____

_____

_____

TRAVEL AGENT _____

PHONE _____

TRAVEL INSURANCE POLICY # _____

HOTLINE NUMBER _____

PERSONAL DATA FOR TRAVELING COMPANION

NAME _____

ADDRESS AND PHONE _____

_____

_____

_____

IN CASE OF EMERGENCY, _____

PLEASE CONTACT _____

_____

_____

_____

MEDICAL INSURANCE POLICY _____

GROUP # _____

FAMILY PHYSICIAN _____

PHONE NUMBER _____

BLOOD GROUP _____

SPECIAL MEDICAL INFO _____

(allergies, etc.) _____

_____

_____

RELIGION _____

S.I.N./SOCIAL SECURITY # _____

PASSPORT NUMBER _____

TICKET NUMBERS _____

_____

_____

TRAVEL AGENT _____

PHONE _____

TRAVEL INSURANCE POLICY # _____

HOTLINE NUMBER _____

MEDICAL SUPPLIES

- ☐ adhesive bandages
- ☐ antihistamine
- ☐ birth control/condoms
- ☐ calamine lotion
- ☐ diarrhea medication
- ☐ headache pills
- ☐ indigestion remedy
- ☐ insect repellent
- ☐ laxative
- ☐ lip balm
- ☐ motion-sickness remedy
- ☐ petroleum jelly
- ☐ prescription drugs
- ☐ vitamins
- ☐ _____
- ☐ _____
- ☐ _____
- ☐ _____

TOILETRIES

- ☐ comb/brush
- ☐ contact lenses/solution/glasses
- ☐ dental floss
- ☐ deodorant
- ☐ feminine hygiene
- ☐ hair care products
- ☐ hair dryer
- ☐ laundry soap
- ☐ nail clippers/file
- ☐ razor/shaving cream
- ☐ shampoo/conditioner
- ☐ shower cap
- ☐ skin lotion
- ☐ sunblock
- ☐ toothbrush/toothpaste
- ☐ _____
- ☐ _____
- ☐ _____
- ☐ _____
- ☐ _____

MISCELLANEOUS

- ☐ adapter/converter
- ☐ address book
- ☐ binoculars
- ☐ birth certificate/identification
- ☐ business cards
- ☐ calculator
- ☐ camera/film/spare batteries
- ☐ credit cards
- ☐ driver's license
- ☐ ear plugs
- ☐ flashlight
- ☐ health insurance
- ☐ insurance policy
- ☐ knapsack/carryall bag
- ☐ money belt
- ☐ passport/visas
- ☐ playing cards
- ☐ portable radio
- ☐ raincoat (folding)
- ☐ slippers
- ☐ small notebook
- ☐ spot remover
- ☐ sun hat/visor
- ☐ sunglasses
- ☐ swimsuit/goggles/bathing cap
- ☐ Swiss Army knife
- ☐ telephone calling card
- ☐ thongs/deck sandals
- ☐ towel/washcloth
- ☐ travel clock
- ☐ travel documents/tickets
- ☐ travel iron
- ☐ traveler's checks
- ☐ umbrella (folding)
- ☐ video camera/tapes/batteries
- ☐ walking shoes
- ☐ _____
- ☐ _____
- ☐ _____

ONE-MONTH CALENDAR

13

ONE-MONTH CALENDAR

MONTH_____   YEAR_____

SUNDAY	MONDAY	TUESDAY	WEDNESDAY	THURSDAY	FRIDAY	SATURDAY

14

Depart From	Date/Time	Arrive At	Date/Time	Comments

Depart From	Date/Time	Arrive At	Date/Time	Comments

Port _____ Description _____
_____
Address/Directions _____
_____
_____
Notes _____
_____
_____
_____
_____

Port _____ Description _____
_____
Address/Directions _____
_____
_____
Notes _____
_____
_____
_____
_____

Port _____ Description _____
_____
Address/Directions _____
_____
_____
Notes _____
_____
_____
_____
_____

Port _____ Description _____

_____

Address/Directions _____

_____

_____

Notes _____

_____

_____

_____

_____

Port _____ Description _____

_____

Address/Directions _____

_____

_____

Notes _____

_____

_____

_____

_____

Port _____ Description _____

_____

Address/Directions _____

_____

_____

Notes _____

_____

_____

_____

_____

Port _____ Description _____

_____

Address/Directions _____

_____

_____

Notes _____

_____

_____

_____

_____

Port _____ Description _____

_____

Address/Directions _____

_____

_____

Notes _____

_____

_____

_____

_____

Port _____ Description _____

_____

Address/Directions _____

_____

_____

Notes _____

_____

_____

_____

_____

Port _____ Description _____

Address/Directions _____

_____

_____

Notes _____

_____

_____

_____

_____

Port _____ Description _____

Address/Directions _____

_____

_____

Notes _____

_____

_____

_____

_____

Port _____ Description _____

Address/Directions _____

_____

_____

Notes _____

_____

_____

_____

_____

Date _____ Time _____
Description _____
_____
_____

Date _____ Time _____
Description _____
_____
_____

Date _____ Time _____
Description _____
_____
_____

Date _____ Time _____
Description _____
_____
_____

Date _____ Time _____
Description _____
_____
_____

Date _____ Time _____
Description _____
_____
_____

Date _____ Time _____
Description _____
_____
_____

Date _____ Time_____
Description_____
_____
_____

Date _____ Time_____
Description_____
_____
_____

Date _____ Time_____
Description_____
_____
_____

Date _____ Time_____
Description_____
_____
_____

Date _____ Time_____
Description_____
_____
_____

Date _____ Time_____
Description_____
_____
_____

Date _____ Time_____
Description_____
_____
_____

Date _____Meal _____
Description_____
_____
_____

Date _____Meal _____
Description_____
_____
_____

Date _____Meal _____
Description_____
_____
_____

Date _____Meal _____
Description_____
_____
_____

Date _____Meal _____
Description_____
_____
_____

Date _____Meal _____
Description_____
_____
_____

Date _____Meal _____
Description_____
_____
_____

Date _____ Meal _____
Description _____
_____
_____

Date _____ Meal _____
Description _____
_____
_____

Date _____ Meal _____
Description _____
_____
_____

Date _____ Meal _____
Description _____
_____
_____

Date _____ Meal _____
Description _____
_____
_____

Date _____ Meal _____
Description _____
_____
_____

Date _____ Meal _____
Description _____
_____
_____

Date _____ Place _____
Description_____
_____
_____
_____

Date _____ Place _____
Description_____
_____
_____
_____

Date _____ Place _____
Description_____
_____
_____
_____

Date _____ Place _____
Description_____
_____
_____
_____

Date _____ Place _____
Description_____
_____
_____
_____

Date _____ Place _____
Description_____
_____
_____
_____

Date _____ Place _____
Description _____
_____
_____
_____

Date _____ Place _____
Description _____
_____
_____
_____

Date _____ Place _____
Description _____
_____
_____
_____

Date _____ Place _____
Description _____
_____
_____
_____

Date _____ Place _____
Description _____
_____
_____
_____

Date _____ Place _____
Description _____
_____
_____
_____

Name_____Cabin # _____
Home Address _____
_____
_____Phone_____

Name_____Cabin # _____
Home Address _____
_____
_____Phone_____

Name_____Cabin # _____
Home Address _____
_____
_____Phone_____

Name_____Cabin # _____
Home Address _____
_____
_____Phone_____

Name_____Cabin # _____
Home Address _____
_____
_____Phone_____

Name_____Cabin # _____
Home Address _____
_____
_____Phone_____

Name_____Cabin # _____
Home Address _____
_____
_____Phone_____

Name _____ Cabin # _____
Home Address _____
_____
_____ Phone _____

Name _____ Cabin # _____
Home Address _____
_____
_____ Phone _____

Name _____ Cabin # _____
Home Address _____
_____
_____ Phone _____

Name _____ Cabin # _____
Home Address _____
_____
_____ Phone _____

Name _____ Cabin # _____
Home Address _____
_____
_____ Phone _____

Name _____ Cabin # _____
Home Address _____
_____
_____ Phone _____

Name _____ Cabin # _____
Home Address _____
_____
_____ Phone _____

Name _____
Address _____
_____
Postal/Zip _____ Phone _____

Name _____
Address _____
_____
Postal/Zip _____ Phone _____

Name _____
Address _____
_____
Postal/Zip _____ Phone _____

Name _____
Address _____
_____
Postal/Zip _____ Phone _____

Name _____
Address _____
_____
Postal/Zip _____ Phone _____

Name _____
Address _____
_____
Postal/Zip _____ Phone _____

Name _____
Address _____
_____
Postal/Zip _____ Phone _____

Name _____
Address _____
_____
Postal/Zip _____ Phone _____

Name _____
Address _____
_____
Postal/Zip _____ Phone _____

Name _____
Address _____
_____
Postal/Zip _____ Phone _____

Name _____
Address _____
_____
Postal/Zip _____ Phone _____

Name _____
Address _____
_____
Postal/Zip _____ Phone _____

Name _____
Address _____
_____
Postal/Zip _____ Phone _____

Name _____
Address _____
_____
Postal/Zip _____ Phone _____

For	Item	Size / Notes

Number	Amount	Date & Place Cashed	Exch. Rate	Number	Amount	Date & Place Cashed	Exch. Rate

Number	Amount	Date & Place Cashed	Exch. Rate	Number	Amount	Date & Place Cashed	Exch. Rate

Item	Amount	Date / Place / Currency Rate	Method

Item	Amount	Date / Place / Currency Rate	Method

RECORD OF PURCHASES

Item	Amount	Date / Place / Currency Rate	Method

Keeping a record of major purchases will help in completing customs forms.
Travelers are also advised to keep all receipts.

Roll #_____ Date Begun _____ Ended _____
Locations _____
_____

Roll #_____ Date Begun _____ Ended _____
Locations _____
_____

Roll #_____ Date Begun _____ Ended _____
Locations _____
_____

Roll #_____ Date Begun _____ Ended _____
Locations _____
_____

Roll #_____ Date Begun _____ Ended _____
Locations _____
_____

Roll #_____ Date Begun _____ Ended _____
Locations _____
_____

Roll #_____ Date Begun _____ Ended _____
Locations _____
_____

Roll #_____ Date Begun _____ Ended _____
Locations _____
_____

Roll #_____ Date Begun _____ Ended _____
Locations _____
_____

Roll #_____ Date Begun _____ Ended _____
Locations _____
_____

Roll #_____ Date Begun _____ Ended _____
Locations _____
_____

Roll #_____ Date Begun _____ Ended _____
Locations _____
_____

Roll #_____ Date Begun _____ Ended _____
Locations _____
_____

Roll #_____ Date Begun _____ Ended _____
Locations _____
_____

Roll #_____ Date Begun _____ Ended _____
Locations _____
_____

Roll #_____ Date Begun _____ Ended _____
Locations _____
_____

Roll #_____ Date Begun _____ Ended _____
Locations _____
_____

Roll #_____ Date Begun _____ Ended _____
Locations _____
_____

DIARY

DATE: PLACE:

DATE: PLACE:

DIARY

DATE: PLACE:

DIARY

DATE: _____ PLACE: _____
_____
_____
_____
_____
_____
_____
_____
_____
_____
_____
_____
_____
_____
_____
_____
_____
_____
_____
_____
_____
_____
_____
_____
_____
_____

DIARY

DATE: PLACE:

DIARY

DATE: _____ PLACE: _____

_____
_____
_____
_____
_____
_____
_____
_____
_____
_____
_____
_____
_____
_____
_____
_____
_____
_____
_____
_____
_____
_____
_____
_____
_____

DIARY

DATE: _____ PLACE: _____

_____
_____
_____
_____
_____
_____
_____
_____
_____
_____
_____
_____
_____
_____
_____
_____
_____
_____
_____
_____
_____
_____
_____
_____
_____
_____
_____

DIARY

DATE: _____ PLACE: _____

_____

_____

_____

_____

_____

_____

_____

_____

_____

_____

_____

_____

_____

_____

_____

_____

_____

_____

_____

_____

_____

_____

_____

DIARY

DATE: _____ PLACE: _____

_____

_____

_____

_____

_____

_____

_____

_____

_____

_____

_____

_____

_____

_____

_____

_____

_____

_____

_____

_____

_____

_____

DATE: PLACE:

DIARY

DATE: PLACE:

DATE: PLACE:

DIARY

DATE: PLACE:

DIARY

DATE: PLACE:

DIARY

DATE: PLACE:

DATE: _____   PLACE: _____

_____

_____

_____

_____

_____

_____

_____

_____

_____

_____

_____

_____

_____

_____

_____

_____

_____

_____

_____

_____

_____

_____

_____

DIARY

DATE: PLACE:

DATE: PLACE:

DIARY

DATE: PLACE:

DIARY

DATE: PLACE:

DIARY

DATE: PLACE:

DATE: PLACE:

DIARY

DATE: PLACE:

_____

_____

_____

_____

_____

_____

_____

_____

_____

_____

_____

_____

_____

_____

_____

_____

_____

_____

_____

_____

_____

_____

_____

_____

_____

DIARY

DATE: _____ PLACE: _____

_____

_____

_____

_____

_____

_____

_____

_____

_____

_____

_____

_____

_____

_____

_____

_____

_____

_____

_____

_____

_____

_____

_____

DIARY

DATE: PLACE:

DATE: PLACE:

DIARY

DATE: _____   PLACE: _____

_____
_____
_____
_____
_____
_____
_____
_____
_____
_____
_____
_____
_____
_____
_____
_____
_____
_____
_____
_____
_____
_____
_____
_____
_____
_____
_____

DATE: _____ PLACE: _____

_____

_____

_____

_____

_____

_____

_____

_____

_____

_____

_____

_____

_____

_____

_____

_____

_____

_____

_____

_____

_____

_____

_____

_____

DIARY

DATE: PLACE:

DATE: PLACE:

DIARY

DATE: PLACE:

DIARY

DATE: _____   PLACE: _____
_____
_____
_____
_____
_____
_____
_____
_____
_____
_____
_____
_____
_____
_____
_____
_____
_____
_____
_____
_____
_____
_____
_____
_____
_____

DIARY

DATE: PLACE:

LINEAR MEASURE

1 millimetre	0.039 inch
1 centimetre = 10 mm	0.394 inch
1 decimetre = 10 cm	3.94 inches
1 metre = 10 dm	1.094 yards
1 decametre = 10 m	10.94 yards
1 hectometre = 100 m	109.4 yards
1 kilometre = 1,000 m	0.6214 mile

SQUARE MEASURE

1 square centimetre	0.155 sq. inch
1 square metre	1.196 sq. yards
1 are = 100 sq. metres	119.6 sq. yards
1 hectare = 100 ares	2.471 acres
1 square kilometre	0.386 sq. mile

CUBIC MEASURE

1 cubic centimetre	0.061 cu. inch
1 cubic metre	1.308 cu. yards

CAPACITY MEASURE *(British conversions)*

1 millilitre	0.002 pint
1 centilitre = 10 ml	0.018 pint
1 decilitre = 10 cl	0.176 pint
1 litre = 10 dl	1.76 pints
1 decalitre = 10l	2.20 gallons
1 hectolitre = 100l	2.75 bushels
1 kilolitre = 1,000l	3.44 quarters

WEIGHT

1 milligram	0.015 grain
1 centigram = 10 mg	0.154 grain
1 decigram = 10 cg	1.543 grain
1 gram = 10 dg	15.43 grain
1 decagram = 10 g	5.64 drams
1 hectogram = 100 g	3.527 ounces
1 kilogram = 1,000 g	2.205 pounds
1 tonne (metric ton) = 1,000 kg	0.984 (long) ton

Simplified Temperature Conversion: $(c \times 2) + 30 = F$; $(F - 32) \div 2 = C$.
Celsius or Centigrade: water boils at 100° and freezes at 0°.
Fahrenheit: water boils (under standard conditions) at 212° and freezes at 32°.

WOMEN'S CLOTHING

Dresses, Suits, Coats, Sweaters, etc

Canada / US	8	10	12	14	16	18
UK	10	12	14	16	18	20
Cont. Europe	38	40	42	44	46	48
Australia	10	12	14	16	18	20

Shoes

Canada / US	5	5½	6	6½	7	7½	8	8½	9	9½	10
UK	3½	4	4½	5	5½	6	6½	7	7½	8	8½
Cont. Europe	35	36	36	37	37	38	38	39	39	40	40
France	35	35	36	37	38	38	39	39	40	41	42
Australia	5	5½	6	6½	7	7½	8	8½	9	9½	10

MEN'S CLOTHING

Suits, Jackets, Sweaters, etc

Canada / US / UK	34	35	36	37	38	39	40	41	42
Cont. Europe	44	46	48	49½	51	52½	54	55½	57
Australia	12	14		16		18		20	

Shirts

Canada / US / UK	14½	15	15½	16	16½	17	17½	18
Cont. Europe	37	38	39	41	42	43	44	45
Australia	37	38	39	41	42	43	44	45

Shoes

Canada / US	7	8	9	10	11	12	13
UK	6	7	8	9	10	11	12
Cont. Europe	40	41	42	43	44½	46	47
Australia	6	7	8	9	10	11	12

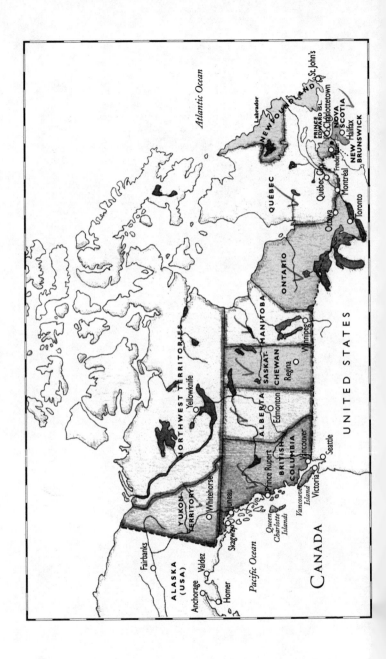

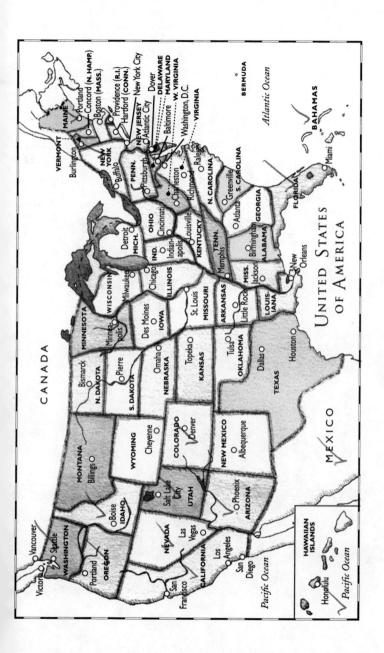

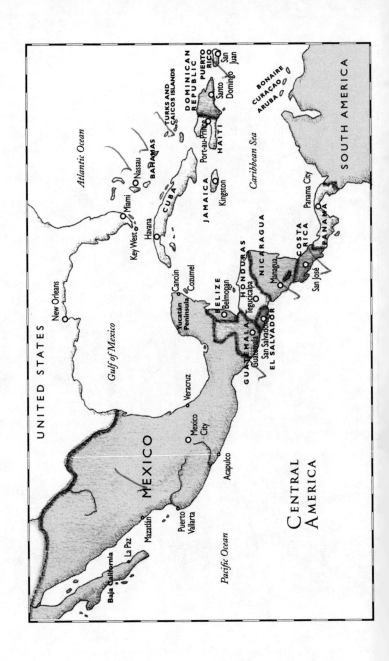

GUADELOUPE
DOMINICA
MARTINIQUE
ST. LUCIA
ST. VINCENT
BARBADOS
GRENADA
TRINIDAD

Caracas

VENEZUELA

Georgetown
Paramaribo
Cayenne

GUIANA
SURINAME
FR. GUIANA

Bogotá

COLOMBIA

Quito

ECUADOR

PERU

Lima

B R A Z I L

La Paz

BOLIVIA

Brasilia

Rio de Janeiro

Pacific Ocean

PARAGUAY

São Paulo

Asunción

Santiago

A R G E N T I N A

URUGUAY

Buenos Aires

Montevideo

Atlantic Ocean

CHILE

**SOUTH
AMERICA**

Falkland
Islands

Tierra del Fuego

EUROPE &
RUSSIAN
FEDERATION

SWEDEN

FINLAND

Helsinki

NORWAY

Tallinn

ESTONIA

Oslo   Stockholm

Riga

LATVIA

RUSSIAN
FEDERATION

Moscow

Faroe Islands

Shetland Islands

LITHUANIA

Vilnius

RUS. FED.

Minsk

SCOTLAND

DENMARK

Copenhagen

BELORUSSIA

N. IRELAND

Amsterdam

POLAND

Kiev

Dublin

NETHERLANDS

Berlin

Warsaw

ENGLAND

London

GERMANY

BELGIUM

Brussels

LUXEMBOURG

UKRAINE

REPUBLIC
OF
IRELAND

WALES

Prague

CZECH
REPUBLIC

SLOVAKIA

Bratislava

MOLDAVIA

LIECHTENSTEIN

Vienna

Budapest

Kishinev

Paris

AUSTRIA

HUNGARY

ROMANIA

Bern

SWITZERLAND

FRANCE

Ljubljana

SLOVENIA

Zagreb

CROATIA

YUGOSLAVIA

Bucharest

Atlantic Ocean

BOSNIA-
HERZEGOVINA

Belgrade

BULGARIA

Sofia

Marseilles

Genoa

ANDORRA

Corsica

I
T
A
L
Y

Rome

Tirane

MACEDONIA

Istanbul

Porto

PORTUGAL

Madrid

Barcelona

Sardinia

GREECE

Valencia

Balearic
Islands

Lisbon

SPAIN

Mediterranean Sea

Málaga

Sicily

Athens

Cádiz

Crete

Gibraltar

Tunis

Casablanca

A F R I C A

90

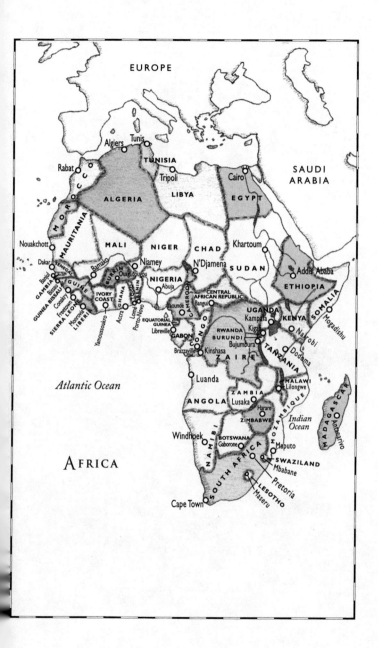

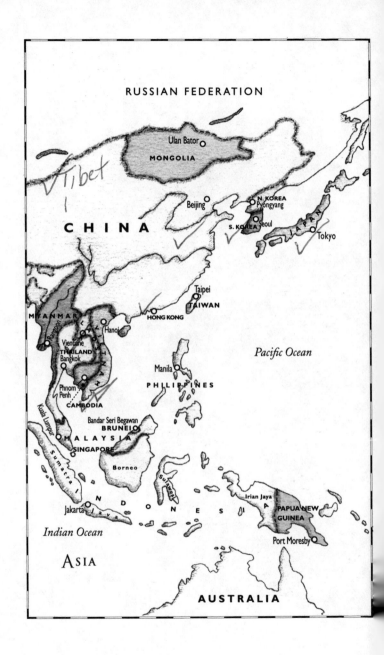

RUSSIAN FEDERATION

Ulan Bator ○

MONGOLIA

Tibet

C H I N A

Beijing ○

N. KOREA
Pyongyang ○
S. KOREA ○ Seoul

JAPAN

Tokyo ○

MYANMAR

Yangon

Hanoi ○
Vientiane ○
THAILAND
Bangkok ○

Phnom
Penh ○
CAMBODIA

Kuala Lumpur
MALAYSIA
SINGAPORE

Sumatra

Jakarta ○

J a v a

Taipei ○
TAIWAN

HONG KONG ○

Manila ○

PHILIPPINES

Pacific Ocean

Bandar Seri Begawan ○
BRUNEI

Borneo

Sulawesi

I   N   D   O   N   E   S   I   A

Irian Jaya

PAPUA NEW
GUINEA

Port Moresby ○

Indian Ocean

ASIA

AUSTRALIA

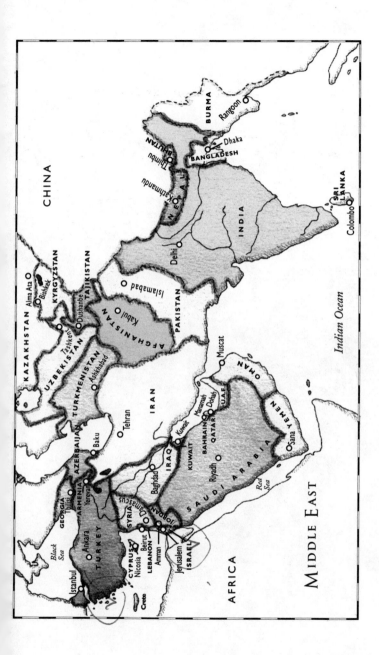

MIDDLE EAST

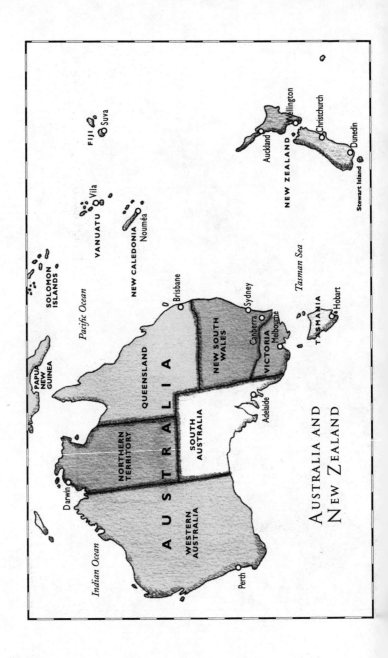

AUSTRALIA AND
NEW ZEALAND